AF482140

Works of
Ralph Green

The Iron Hand Press In America

A History of The Platen Jobber

On Making A Printing Press

Published by
Ye Olde Printery

A Reprint Published by
Ye Olde Printery
5815 Cherokee Drive
Cincinnati, Ohio 45243

Printed in the U.S.A.
1981

Library of Congress Catalog Number 81-51378
ISBN: 0-932606-02-4

Preface

Those of us who are hobby printers and students of printing history are particularly eager to avail ourselves of every bit of useful information about antique printing presses. Among the books most sought after are those written by Ralph Green.

Mr. Green was a historian and printer-hobbyist. His books are highly regarded; their value as important reference works is well known. Ralph Green was a skilled draftsman and a careful scholar. A civil engineer by profession, he brought the same qualities to his work in building printing presses that he did as a builder of bridges and water towers. Plans for a working model of the authentic hand press presently in use at Colonial Williamsburg were drawn up by Ralph Green.

Perhaps because of his modesty, only 160 copies of "Iron Hand Press" were printed in 1948. There were 495 copies of "A History of the Platen Jobber", his second book, published in 1953. However, for his third book, "On Making a Printing Press", only 170 were printed.

Mr. Green's death in 1960, at age 67, meant that there would be no more wonderful books coming from this enterprising and hard-working researcher. Yet these meticulous works on the history of the American printing press deserve to be available to all those who seek their very informative pages. Although we cannot increase Mr. Green's legacy, we can share his great knowledge with others by reprinting his books.

We wish to thank C. Prentiss Smith and E.H. Mundell for making available materials that would enable this project to become a reality.

The

Iron Hand Press

In America

The

Iron Hand Press

In America

RALPH GREEN

with illustrations by Robert Galvin
after drawings by Ralph Green

Rowayton, Connecticut
1948

The day of the all wooden "common" printing press was drawing to a close. It had served well, and without the benefit of much improvement, for over 300 years. The time was ripe for a change. Iron for machinery, and primitive machine tools paved the way for improvement in printing presses. Over in England in 1800, Charles, Third Earl Stanhope, had invented and caused to be manufactured in numbers, an all-iron printing press, which to the English printers was a vast improvement over the wooden press. It had sufficient power to accomodate a platen of double the size of the wooden platen, and so could print a full form at one impression. The wooden presses had been of the "two pull" variety, with the platen half the size of the form, and requiring two pulls of the bar to print a full sheet.

It was not until 1811 that the first Stanhope press appeared in this country. Its merits must have been recognized, as within the next few years the daily papers of New York were being printed on Stanhope presses. The advantages of a more powerful and faster press appealed particularly to the newspaper printers, who had a limited time to get their papers on the streets. It was only natural that some ingenious American would turn his attention to the manufacture of an iron press. George Clymer of Philadelphia was the man and he named his press the Columbian.

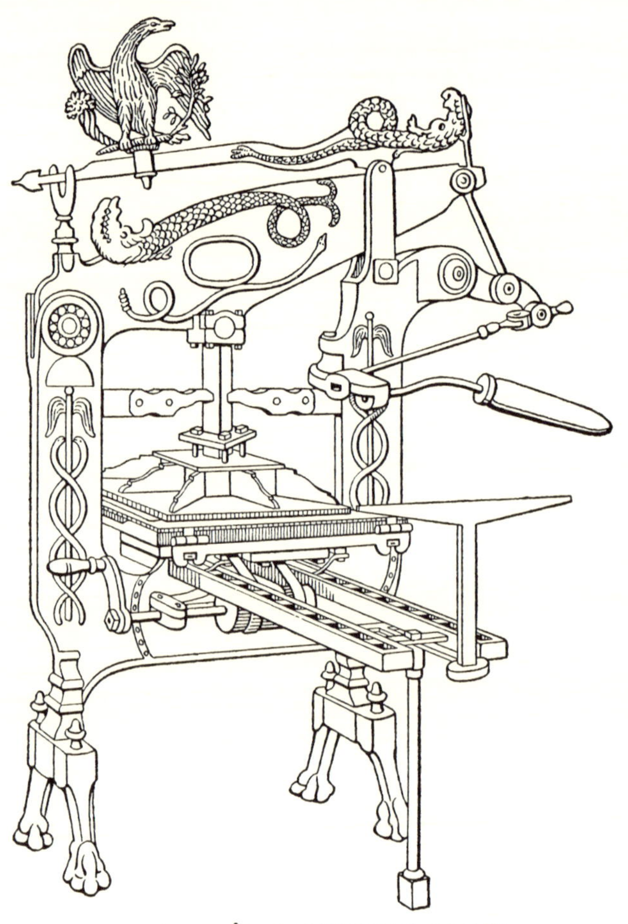

CLYMER'S COLUMBIAN PRESS

GEORGE CLYMER

& HIS COLUMBIAN PRESS

Clymer was born in Bucks County, Pennsylvania, in 1754, the son of a farmer. At an early age he showed great mechanical skill, and after learning the carpenter and cabinetmakers' trade, he continued devoting a good part of his time to improvements in machinery. He constructed a pump which was superior to any yet made, and which was used to clear the water from within the cofferdams of the first permanent bridge across the Schuylkill River at Philadelphia. He turned his attention to the printing press in 1797, and made minor improvements in the wooden press. In 1805 he was listed in the Philadelphia directory as a press

maker, and in 1813 as a "patent printing press manufacturer." Early patent office records, however, do not
list Clymer or his press. We may infer that between
those dates he worked out his design for an iron press.
The completed press in its final form appeared in
1813. It is doubtful whether he had even seen a Stanhope press, or if he had, the English press did little in
influencing his design. The general arrangement and
mechanical details had little in common with the
Stanhope.

The Columbian was the first press to eliminate the
screw. The action consisted of a heavy iron crossbeam
pivoted at one end, and pulled down at the other end
by means of an ingenious toggle mechanism. Midway
of the beam, where the screw was normally located in
the older presses, was a vertical member, which was
depressed by the beam and which in turn forced the
platen down on the paper. At the top of the press, a
cast iron eagle, perched on a horizontal bar, served as
a counterweight to assist in raising the platen after the
impression. The main castings of the press were orna-
mented with dragons, snakes, and other devices. There
was never a press, before or since, which carried so
much ornamentation.

There are no exact figures as to the number of these
presses Clymer manufactured. They were first intro-

duced in Philadelphia and it was reported that William Fry of that city had a row of them. Munsell states that nearly all the papers in New York adopted them. An early engraving of the Columbian indicates on its name plate that press number 25 was made in 1816.

The sale of his presses, however, proved a disappointment to Clymer. It was quite possible that the market became saturated before the smaller printers were aware of the advantages of the press. The price of $400 was too great an investment when it was possible to buy a wooden press for less than half that amount. Only the larger printing houses could afford such a press.

Early in 1817 we find Clymer, at the age of 63, going to England to seek a wider field for the sale of his presses. It must have taken courage for an American to invade a market which was already well served by not only the Stanhope, but by two or three other new model presses. Clymer was well equipped with testimonials from American printers. He arranged with an English press maker, R. W. Cope, to handle the manufacture of the Columbian, and a patent was granted him on November 1, 1817.

From the first his press was well received by the English printers. Trials indicated that it had greater power than the Stanhope. The absence of the screw, with a corresponding decrease in frictional area, probably accounted for its easy working. Two English printers' manuals, published a few years later, state that in printing large wood blocks, with heavy black areas, the new press was unsurpassed. Clymer retained the name Columbian, and also the American eagle counterweight perched majestically on the top bar. These features acted in no way as a drawback to the purchase of the press by English printers, who apparently were attracted by the ornamental appearance of the machine.

About 1827 the firm of Clymer & Dixon was organized to handle the manufacture of the press. George Clymer died in London, August 27, 1834, at the age of 80, but the business was continued for a great many years after his death. After the expiration of the patent, other firms commenced the manufacture and sale of the Columbian. Its popularity was such that English supply houses listed it until a few years ago. The design was also copied on the continent, and during the last century, at one time or another, Columbians were made in Holland, France and Germany. The eagle was replaced, however, by an ornamental urn.

Clymer's press, while better than its predecessors, did not have any particular effect on the design of

American presses which followed. Its type of mecha-
anism was unique. Later presses were more powerful,
and yet were lighter in weight.

To the best of the writer's knowledge, there are no
original Columbians in this country. Probably the
25 or 30 made before 1817 were scrapped many years
ago. There are, however, two or three good English
examples in America, but these were made some years
after Clymer's death.

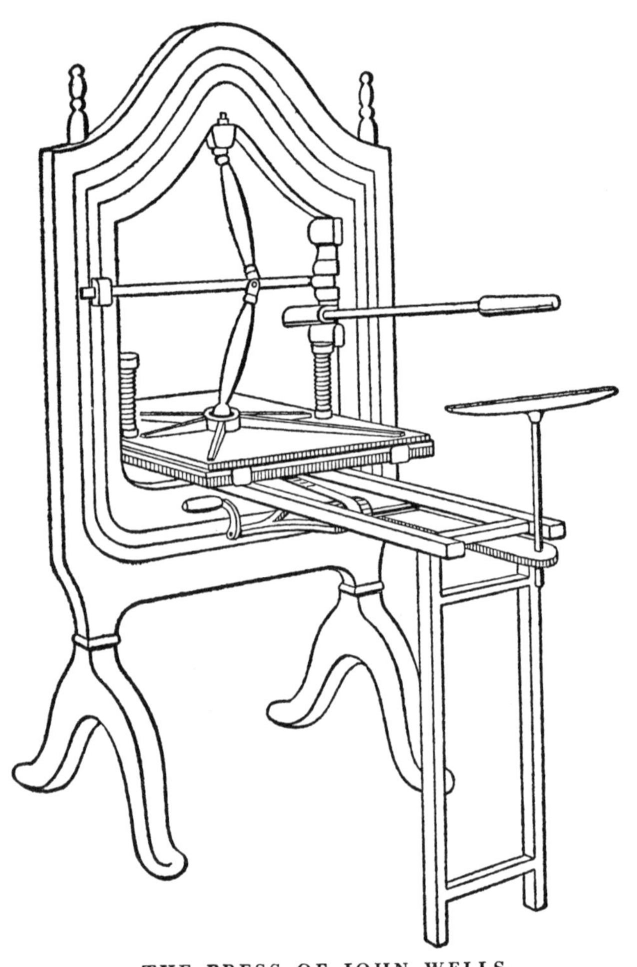

THE PRESS OF JOHN WELLS

JOHN I. WELLS

& THE TOGGLE JOINT

John I. Wells of Hartford, Connecticut, a Quaker and originally a cabinetmaker, turned to the making of ink for printers, some time before 1815. In the manufacture of linseed oil for this purpose, he had made use of a press for extracting the oil, which incorporated a simple form of a toggle joint. Realizing the need for an improved printing press, he at first adapted the toggle joint to a wooden press. As might be expected, the power was too great for the wooden frame and his experiments were not a success. He later used iron throughout in the construction of his press, and applied for a patent, which was granted February 8, 1819.

The Wells press sold for $350 and apparently enjoyed a reasonably good sale. It was on the market only a few years, however, when the Smith and Rust presses appeared in New York. The competition cut into Wells' business and although quite a number of his presses were sold, they did not reach the popularity of later designs. Probably his location in Hartford did not offer as good an opportunity for sales as that of his competitors in New York. Few changes were made in the appearance of his press, and when he died in 1833, manufacture ceased.

To Wells, however, can be given the credit for introducing the first true, simple toggle joint press. His followers adopted his idea and improved upon it. **C. L.** Adams' *Typographia*, a printer's textbook which appeared in 1828, contains a long letter from Wells written in the same year. In it Wells complains that Peter Smith, who later brought out the well known Smith press, had carefully examined several Wells presses in New York and, as a result, obtained a patent on a somewhat similar press. Wells was a believer in long toggle levers, and stated that the height of the toggle in his press gave it unusual power. His original presses used a heavy cast iron ball as a counterweight. It wasn't until other press makers had adopted the use of springs to raise the platen, that

Wells realized the awkwardness of his heavy counterweight. He thereupon changed to the use of springs.
Printers complained that his press was difficult to
operate because the bar was located on the off side
and required extra reach to manage it. This was
corrected, however, and the bar was moved to the near
side on later models.

The Wells press had a very light platen, as compared to platen construction on Washington presses
of a later date, and the large cast iron frame of his press
was not as strong as that of his successors. Doubtless
the need for extreme strength of construction was not
realized in Wells' time, as printers had been accus-
tomed to the limitations of the wooden press. But we
must give Wells full credit for introducing the form
of hand press which was the pattern followed by his
successors. What little has been written on this subject
gives Wells only casual mention. He deserves more.

There are a number of Wells presses still in existence. The author knows of five, and there may be
as many more tucked away in museums or old printing offices in the east. The Smithsonian Institution
has a perfect specimen of one of the early models.

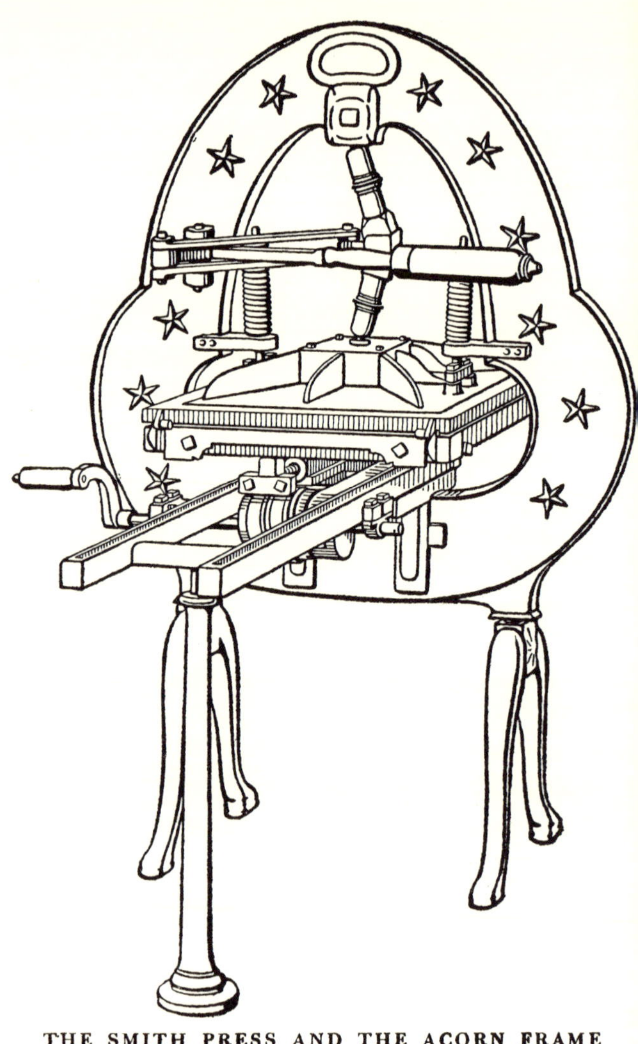

THE SMITH PRESS AND THE ACORN FRAME

& THE HOE COMPANY

Robert Hoe, with his two brothers-in-law, Peter and Matthew Smith, formed a partnership in 1805 for the manufacture of printer's wood goods, such as stands, cases, etc. Within a short time they undertook to make presses, and developed a good business in the sale of wooden presses of the "common wood press" type. The firm was progressive and after the advent of the Columbian and Wells presses, realized that the iron press had come to stay.

Peter Smith obtained two patents. Of the first one, dated December 29, 1821, all records have been lost and we can't even guess what kind of a press it covered.

The patent office drawing for the second, granted April 6, 1822, is still in existence, and shows a strange species of mechanism which was far from anything like the well-known Smith press which followed. When the Hoe firm really got started with manufacture, the press they produced had a toggle joint like that of the Wells. The bar attachment was different, however, and in that respect was not an exact copy of the Wells. The frame, of heavy cast iron construction, was somewhat like an acorn in outline, whereas the frame of the Wells press had parallel sides. The bar was on the near side, where it ought to be, and springs were used to raise the platen. Others before had him used springs, so this feature was not new.

Matthew Smith died in 1820, and his brother, Peter, died in 1823, shortly after his press was put on the market. Robert Hoe became the sole owner of the business, which was carried on under the name of Robert Hoe & Company. The Smith press was heavier and stronger than the Wells, and enjoyed a good sale. When the Hoe Company took over Samuel Rust's business in 1835, and acquired the Washington patent, the acorn frame was abandoned and the Smith toggle mechanism was adapted to the newer and better Washington frame, of which we shall say more later. Although the Hoe firm, after 1835, made two types of hand presses, they admitted that the Smith toggle was inferior to the true Washington type. It was not until 1880 that manufacture of the Smith press was discontinued.

Peter Smith has been given more credit than he deserves. On the strength of a patent of doubtful value, a press was produced which contained no new features worthy of comment. The business ability of the Hoe firm, together with good workmanship, and a heavy, strong design were probably accountable for the success of the press and its long life on the market.

A number of examples of the original Smith press with acorn frame are still in existence. Two of them are actually being used for proofing and for short runs. Of the later Smith design, with Washington frame, there are still more scattered around the country, which have been successfully kept out of the hands of the junk man.

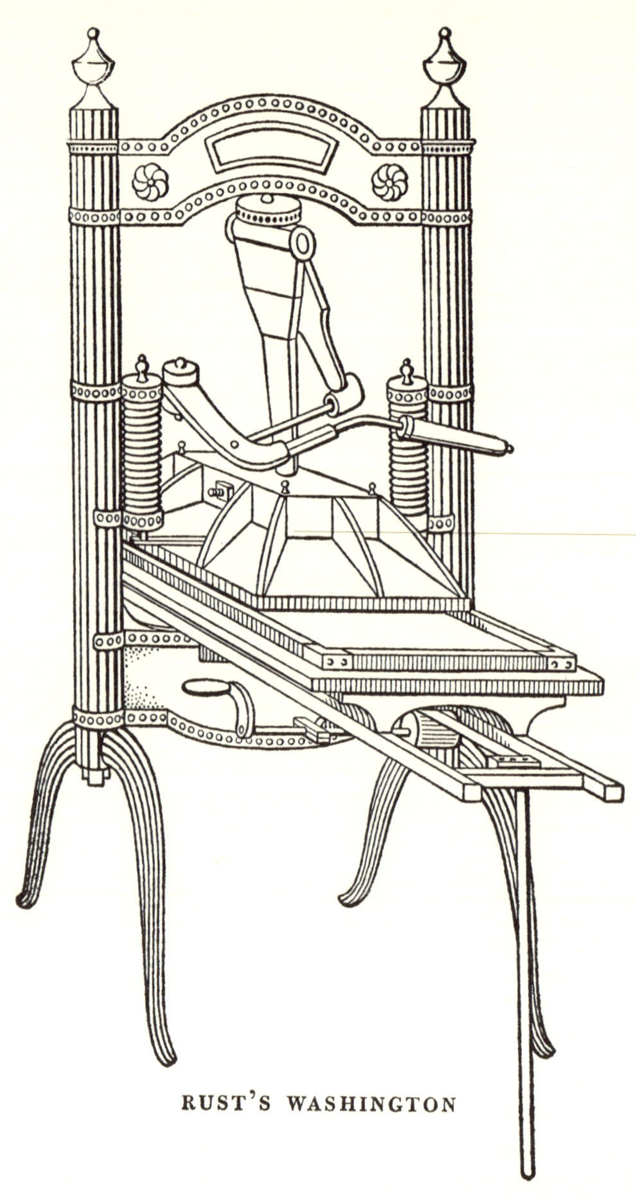

RUST'S WASHINGTON

SAMUEL RUST

& THE WASHINGTON PRESS

We know very little about Samuel Rust of New York, where and when he was born, or what his original occupation may have been. There is some indication, however, that he was not a young man when he invented the Washington press, as he was making plans to retire in the early thirties.

He is first encountered in the New York directory of 1817, where he is listed as a printer in the rear of 19 Mott Street. We may infer that business was not too good, as he seems to have moved four times in four years. In 1819 and 1820 he is listed as "printer and grocer," a combination uncommon in our times.

His first patent was granted May 13, 1821. The patent office reports that all record of this patent has been lost. From actual examples of his early presses, and from descriptions in advertisements, we may infer that this patent covered his "figure 4" toggle, which was an improvement on the simple toggle of the Wells press, in that it provided greater leverage in the application of the power. Otherwise, the press was similar in appearance to the Smith. The heavy frame, however, did not look quite as much like an acorn. Rust named his product the Washington Press.

At this period he seems to have had a partner, as the old fashioned brass name plates on his presses stated "manufactured by Rust & Turney." Turney seems to have dropped out in the early thirties.

Rust's second patent, and probably of more value than his first, is dated April 17, 1829. The patent office can supply a drawing applicable to this patent, but it is not very informative. It seems to indicate details of both the figure 4 toggle and the improved frame. Patent office specifications are not available. It is the writer's understanding that this drawing was made many years after the patent was granted, and before the destruction of the patent office models, which at one time were necessary for the purpose of obtaining a patent. Probably the drawing was made from the model, which may have incorporated the details of both the earlier and later patents.

An 1834 advertisement of the Rust press clearly indicates that the frame was a new improvement, so we may be safe in assuming that the 1829 patent applied to the improved frame only.

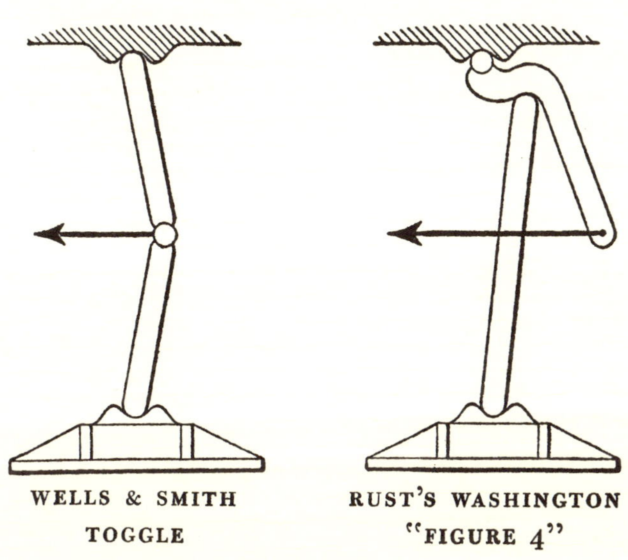

WELLS & SMITH
TOGGLE

RUST'S WASHINGTON
"FIGURE 4"

While Rust, doubtless, was not a structural or mechanical engineer, he must have had some understanding of the stresses in the main frame of a printing press. The older heavy cast iron frame was not only wasteful of material, but was awkward to transport over great distances, at a time when transportation was

ACORN CAST IRON FRAME

difficult. Rust's newly patented frame eliminated the one piece heavy casting and replaced it by two much smaller cast iron beams and two vertical rods. The

The Iron Hand Press - 18

new design was structurally sound. The two castings
acted as simple beams, one at the bottom and one at

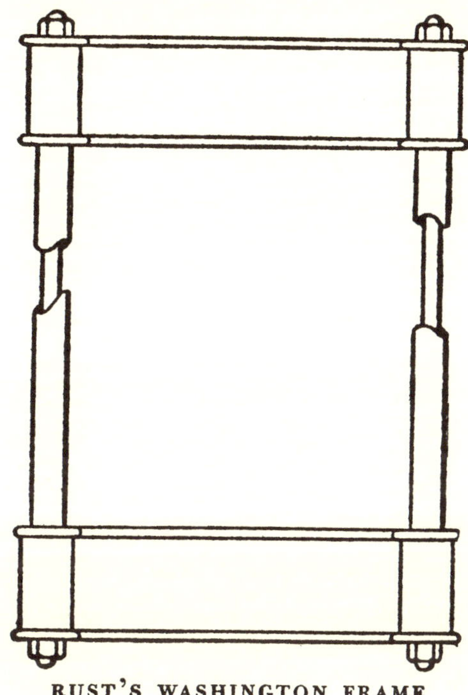

RUST'S WASHINGTON FRAME

the top of the frame, and the rods acted as tension
members, connecting the beams. In order to separate
the top and bottom beams, the rods were enclosed in

19 - *Rust & the Washington Press*

light weight and hollow cast iron fluted columns. The new frame had the further advantage that it could be taken apart for shipment.

Rust claimed that his new style frame weighed only half as much as the acorn cast iron frame, and was four times as strong. These claims were exaggerations but the new frame was definitely lighter and stronger than the old style.

The Washington hand press had now reached its final form, which it was destined to keep until its manufacture was discontinued, almost a century later. Mechanically and structurally, it was as nearly perfect a hand press as has ever been designed.

About 1834 Rust decided to retire. The Hoe people, realizing that the Washington was much superior to their Smith press, had on a number of occasions tried to purchase Rust's patent, but Rust had no love for his chief competitor and wouldn't sell. When it was known that Rust was retiring, a young member of the Hoe firm, John Colby, approached Rust and stated that as he, too, didn't like the methods of the Hoe people, he wanted to quit them and go in business for himself. A bargain was made, and Colby took over Rust's business. In a short time, however, Colby moved everything over to the Hoe plant, and the Washington press was made thereafter by the Hoe people who, if they couldn't get the patent in one way, they could in another.

Rust's reputation as an inventor may be somewhat clouded, as his type of improved frame had been used in England five or ten years before the date of his second patent. A man named Cogger introduced to the London market, sometime between 1818 and 1824, an iron press with cast iron beams, held together by wrought iron side rods. In Cogger's case, however, these rods extended below the frame and were attached to a foundation piece, thus serving as legs for the press. The frame of the Cogger may have been quite satisfactory, but the press as a whole was not, and did not survive many years. The arrangement for obtaining the power caused too rapid wear of certain parts. We can only speculate as to whether Rust saw, or heard of, a Cogger press before taking out his 1829 patent. Due to the limited use of the Cogger press, and its unpopularity, the writer believes Rust probably did not see one. Furthermore, Rust used his side rods for the purpose of only holding the two crossbeams together and not, as Cogger did, in providing a complete side member for the support of the press.

Only slight changes were made in the appearance of the Washington as the years passed, but none in the principle of operation. The platens and frames became heavier and the ornamental work slowly disappeared until, after the turn of the century, when Hoe discontinued making hand presses, the Washington was a very plain press indeed, without a bit of ornamentation.

Almost all old iron presses are erroneously called Washingtons, whether or not they have the true figure 4 toggle and the improved frame. Owners of old Wells, Columbian and Smith presses seem to have a hazy idea that the iron press was intoduced in the time of George Washington and such presses may be of Revolutionary day vintage. Actually their presses may be older than the Washington type, but not as old as their owners would like to believe.

The name Washington, as applied to the iron press, has been in common use for over a century, but Samuel Rust has been forgotten. He invented and perfected a tool which, if its long and useful life is considered, has been of more importance and greater help to the country printer than any one item in the office.

OTHER IRON PRESSES

& THEIR MAKERS

So far, we have described only four different presses. There were many others. The history of the hand press can hardly be complete without mention of Adam Ramage of Philadelphia. Ramage's presses, however, were largely of wood, and his popular types retained the screw as the means of applying the power to the platen. Consequently the typical Ramage press does not have a place in the story of the development of the iron press. Ramage, however, made other presses which should be mentioned.

In 1818 Ramage, while still making wooden presses (but with iron beds and platens), introduced the

Ruthven to this county. This press had been patented in the United States as early as 1813 by John Ruthven, who made presses in Scotland. Ramage apparently made arrangements for manufacture in America and a number were produced, just how many we do not know. The press was unlike any made before or since. The bed and form were fixed in place, and the platen could be rolled on wheels from its position over the form, to the back of the press, thus allowing the tympan to be operated. A toggle joint below the bed was so arranged as to grip the edges of the platen when in its forward position, and force it down on the tympan. The main frame of the press was of wood, and the bar, which moved in a vertical plane, was located at the front of the press. In operating the press, the bar was depressed, and, as considerable force was required, it was necessary for the pressman to retain a firm grip, for if the bar should fly up it was quite likely to knock his teeth out, an accident which was not at all uncommon. There is one good example of a Ruthven extant, still being used for proofing in a small eastern Pennsylvania printing office.

As the iron hand press became increasingly popular, Ramage evidently realized his wooden frame presses were becoming outdated. In 1834 he patented an iron hand press which he called the Philadelphia.

The Iron Hand Press - 24

The toggle was a compromise between the Wells type and the Washington, in fact it was similar to Rust's "figure 4" toggle, stretched out to appear to be like the simple Wells arrangement. The patent, however, based its claims on the type of frame used. Instead of a cast iron beam for a head, and wrought iron round side rods, Ramage made the frame of heavy bars about four inches by one inch in size. At a height about even with the center of the toggle, these bars sloped inward at a 45 degree angle and met at the top, thus providing a triangular frame for the head. This was really an advance in press construction as it utilized the principle of a truss instead of a solid beam. It had one disadvantage, however, as the frame could not be dismantled for transportation. This press deserved a better future. Its sale was limited, however, as Ramage was then 62 years old and probably not as aggressive in his selling as the Hoe Company. Ramage died in 1850 but his successor, Frederick Bronstrup, continued the manufacture of the Philadelphia until shortly after the Civil War. There is a good example of this press in the Museum of Science and Industry in Chicago.

One other type of iron press must be mentioned. As early as 1836, James Maxwell of New York believed that the hand press could be improved if the

25 - *Other Iron Hand Presses*

toggle were placed below the bed, and so arranged that the bed would be pushed upward against the platen. The chief advantage appears to have been in the reduced height of the frame. The press was named the Eagle, and it is doubtful whether many were sold. A man named Jones, living in Cincinnati, revived the press in 1851, and advertised it as an entirely new idea in press construction. About the same time, or shortly after, Charles Foster, who had been working for the Cincinnati Type Foundry as a machinist in the hand press department, obtained a patent, dated October 5, 1852, covering the same kind of an arrangement. Foster, shortly afterwards, moved to Philadelphia, where he commenced manufacture of his patent press. In 1857, the Hoe Company bought Foster's patent and brought out the press under the name of Improved Washington press, with the expectation that it would supplant the original Rust Washington. This was not the case, however, as the original Washington had too firm a hold in its field and about 1868 the Hoe people discontinued their improved press.

No further attempts were made to improve the Washington and the design became practically standardized. Small country newspapers offered a big market for the press even into the eighties and nineties.

The Iron Hand Press - 26

Iron hand presses built after 1900 were used almost entirely by photoengravers for proofing cuts. In this field their life was short, however, as after World War I the cylinder proof press supplanted them. The iron hand press had run its life course. Now they are found only in museums and dusty corners of country printing offices, or in the quiet shops of amateurs.

A CHRONOLOGY OF THE

MAKERS OF THE IRON PRESS

In the following table I have attempted to list chronologically the makers of iron hand presses in the United States. Undoubtedly my list is incomplete. There were probably other manufacturers of Washingtons in the second half of the century who sold their presses unlabeled through type foundries or equipment dealers. The letters following the city of manufacture designate the type of press as follows:

a, *True Washington press* e, *Rust's figure 4 toggle*
b, *Rust's Washington frame* f, *Toggle beneath bed*
c, *Cast iron frame* g, *Part wood frame*
d, *Wells-like toggle* h, *Toggle unclassified*

27 - *Other Iron Hand Presses*

The following shortened forms have been used in the list below: *C. T. F.* for *Cincinnati Type Foundry*, and *Hoe* for *R. Hoe & Co.*

1813-17 Columbian, *George Clymer, Philadelphia* c,h
18-21 Ruthven, *Adam Ramage, Philadelphia* f,g
19-33 Wells, *John J. Wells, Hartford, Conn.* c,d
21-29 Washington, *Rust & Turney, N. Y.* c,e
22-35 Stansbury, *C. T. F., Cincinnati* g,h
22-35 Smith, *Hoe, N. Y.* c,d
27-37 Couillard, *Phineas Dow, Boston* c,d
29-32 Washington, *Samuel Rust, N. Y.* a
31-37 Tufts, *Otis Tufts, Boston* c,d
32-59 Adams, *Seth Adams, Boston* c,d
34-51 Smith, *C. T. F., Cincinnati* c,d
34-50 Philadelphia, *Adam Ramage, Phila.* h
35-80 Smith, *Hoe, N. Y.* b,d
35-02 Washington, *Hoe, N. Y.* a
36- ? Eagle, *James Maxwell, N. Y.* b,f
36- ? Austin, *Fred J. Austin, N. Y.* c,d
45- ? Cosfeldt, *F. J. Cosfeldt, Philadelphia* a
45- ? *Worrall & Co., N. Y.* b,d also e
c. 45 Franklin, *Dickinson & Williamson, Cincinnati* c,d
c. 45 American, *Adam Ramage, Philadelphia* b,e
1850-66 Bronstrup, *Fred Bronstrup, Philadelphia* h
c. 50 Sheridan, *B. Sheridan, N. Y.* b,d

1851-99 Washington, *C. T. F., Cincinnati* **a**
  51- *?* Jones, *Guilford & Jones, Cincinnati* **b,f**
  52-57 Foster, *Charles Foster, Philadelphia* **b,f**
  54-66 Taylor, *A. B. Taylor Mfg.Co., N. Y.* **a**
  56- *?* Stansbury, *C. T. F., Cincinnati* **c,h**
  57-68 Improved Washington, *Hoe, N. Y.* **b,f**
  67-76 Taylor, *A. B. Taylor Son & Co., Chicago* **a**
  67-85 Stansbury, *Hoe, N. Y.* **c,h**
  74-92 Washington, *Franklin Type Foundry,*
                                    Cincinnati **a**
  80- *?* Washington, *J. T. Carroll, N. Y.* **a**
  81-91 Madison, *W. G. Walker, Madison, Wis.* **a**
  81-92 Washington, *Palmer & Rey,*
                                    San Francisco **a**
  87-92 Washington, *Marder Luse & Co., Chicago* **a**
  88-93 Washington, *Shniedewend & Lee, Chicago* **a**
  93-03 Washington, *Challenge Machinery Co.,*
                                    Chicago **a**
  95-12 Reliance, *Paul Shniedewend & Co.,*
                                    Chicago **a**
1900-23 Wesel, *F. Wesel Mfg, Co., N. Y.* **a**
c. 00   Porter, *?* , *Muscatine, Iowa* **b,h**
  09-10 Washington, *Morgans & Wilcox Co.,*
                                    Middletown, N. Y. **a**
  12-30 Perfection, *H. B. Rouse & Co., Chicago* **b,h**
c. 13   Reliance, *W. A. Field, Chicago* **a**

29 - *Chronology of Presses*

THIS IS COPY NO.   OF

ONE HUNDRED AND SIXTY COPIES

PRINTED AND BOUND AT

The Press  in Rowayton

MARIAN & BRUCE SWEET

OCTOBER 1948

A History of the Platen Jobber

A HISTORY OF
The Platen Jobber

by

Ralph Green

Author of The Iron Hand Press in America

The Printing Office of Philip Reed

Chicago:1953

INTRODUCTION

THE STUDENT of platen press history will look in vain for any books on the subject. Here and there, in printers' manuals and text books of this century, may be found references to the development of the jobber, but such items are often not reliable, and sources are not given.

The best sources of printing press history are found in the printers' periodicals of the time. Probably the most useful have been:—

American Bookmaker, 1885-1897, New York
American Model Printer, 1879-1885, New York
Chicago Specimen, 1867-1880, Chicago
Chromatic Art Magazine, 1879-1884, New York
Mirror of Typography, 1869-1874, New York
The Printer, 1858-1875, New York
Printer's Circular, 1866-1890, Philadelphia
Proof Sheet, 1867-1882, New York
Quadrat, 1873-1884, Pittsburgh
Rounds' Printers' Cabinet, 1856-1887, Chicago

Patent papers present an accurate record of what the inventor had in mind when he first brought out an improved press. Practically all of the outstanding platen jobbers were protected by patents.

For the rest, items picked up over a period of twenty years, here and there, in papers, periodicals, and books of the last century, helped to fill out the story. Nor can I forget the old time printer who, more than forty years ago told me the story of the job presses of his youth. He lived during the times of the early jobbers and was acquainted with their idiosyncrasies. It was because of his talks that I wanted to learn more of the history of the treadle driven jobber.

ICTURE a typical small printing office in a city of moderate size in the eighteen thirties. The equipment probably consisted of one hand press and some type, and the output was limited to what we now call job work, with an occasional pamphlet, or more rarely, a small book or two. Items as small as cards or tickets frequently were handled, and what a bother it must have been to print a small card on even a medium sized hand press with its large tympan and frisket.

There were two or three makes of small hand presses manufactured for job work, but the principle of operation was just the same as with the larger presses and the printer had to go thru all the motions required in hand press work. The speed could not have been better than 300 per hour, and for larger work was probably considerably less.

One enterprising New York printer offered cards at cut rate prices. He saved up his orders for about a week and then made up one form, containing the type for something like 12, 16, or 24 cards. He used large card stock on the press and afterwards cut it up into the original orders on a crude hand card cutter.

A number of printers realized the inefficiency of the hand press for small work, and a few, with some inventive genius, did something about it. In the forties at least two self-inking card presses were manufactured and enjoyed a limited sale. Their price was high and the quality of their work somewhat less than perfect.

Two men, however, both practical printers, carried on experimental work during this period, which eventually led to fame and fortune. The first job press to be regularly manufactured was produced by Stephen P. Ruggles of Boston. The second successful experimenter was George P. Gordon of New York, the inventor of the well known Gordon platen jobber.

Stephen P. Ruggles

RUGGLES served his apprenticeship in the early twenties and like quite a few other inventive printers, tried his hand at making a power press. This he succeeded in doing and in 1827 completed a cylinder press which may not have been perfect, but it actually worked. Lack of capital prevented its further development.

In 1830 he constructed the first card press to be made in this country, and it was also the first press to receive the card or sheet directly on the platen, without benefit of separate tympan or frisket. This little press was never manufactured however, and Ruggles was afterwards employed in making presses for printing for the blind. He was successful in this work, and later turned again to the making of printing presses.

He completed his so-called Engine Press in 1839 and a patent on the machine was issued to him in November, 1840. This was the first self-inking treadle driven job printing press to be regularly manufactured in this or any other country. It had a chase size of 10 by 14 inches, and didn't look anything like any jobber you've

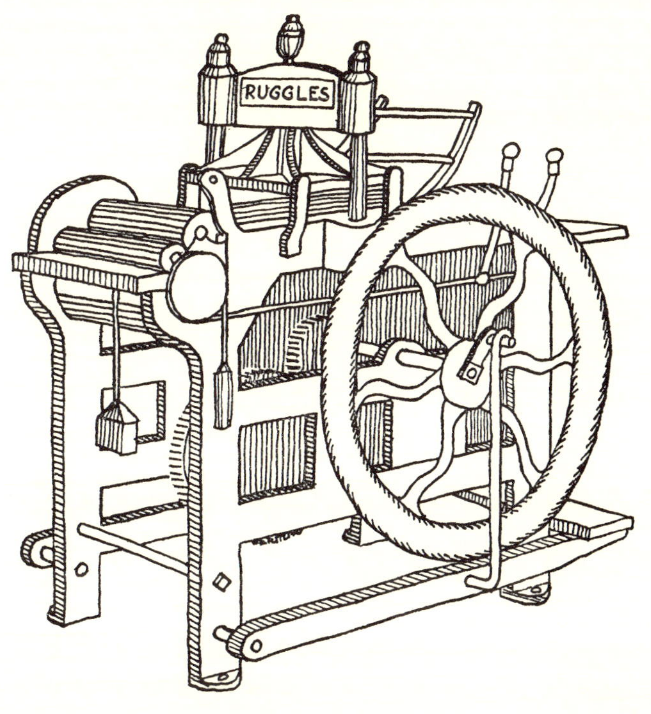

Ruggles' Engine Press of 1840

ever seen. Following the pattern of the hand press, the bed and platen were horizontal, but the type form was above, and the platen was below. In later years it earned the name of the Upside Down press. A tympan carriage, to which the inking rollers were attached, moved back and forth between the form and the platen. A large fountain roller at the back end of the press provided the ink supply, without benefit of ink disk. The speed was 1200 an hour and the press was immediately successful.

Ruggles' method of handling the sale of the press was unique. The selling price was considerably greater than the prices for hand presses used for job work. Altho the speed of the new press was three times as fast as the hand press and only one man was needed to run it instead of two, evidently printers shied away from it because of the cost. With each press sold, Ruggles included the exclusive right to operate his Engine Press in the particular territory or city in which the printer was located. This apparently worked to Ruggles' satisfaction for a short time, but as the merits and advantages of the press became known, there was a greater demand from the large cities where his agreements for exclusive use prohibited sales to other printers. It became necessary for Ruggles to buy back these exclusive rights before the press could be sold in unlimited quantities.

Wooden quoins were used in those days for locking up the forms and the furniture, type, leads, etc. were not made to an exact point system such as we have now. A good tight lockup must have been a necessity, as a loose form could have caused no end of damage by falling down into the tympan and rollers during the operation of the press. The arrangement with the type above the tympan however, did have the advantage of delivering the sheet printed side up.

The patent drawings of the Engine Press indicate a rather complicated mechanism with a great many working parts. Ruggles probably realized that a job press of simpler construction could be produced, and on January 1, 1851, a patent was issued to him covering his Card and Bill Head Press. This press had the distinction of being the first printing press with a vertical bed, a platen hinged below its lower edge, arranged to vibrate or rock back and forth to the form, and so constructed that the sheet could be placed right on the platen and not on a movable tympan. In those three respects it resembled most of the job presses of later years. In appearance, however, it was different.

The bed of the press consisted of a large cylinder with its axis horizontal, and with the front side flattened where the form was attached. The rollers traveled all the way around the bed, and that portion of the cylinder not occupied by the form served as an ink distributing table. Nothing in the way of a vibrating roller was provided and how the ink was distributed laterally, or cross-wise, is a mystery. Probably a hand brayer was used each time fresh ink was applied.

In visualizing the mechanical action of the press it might appear that the bed could not be properly braced or held in a firm position at the time of impression, as the roller arms and rollers, in their travel around the cylinder, would interfere with such bracing. To overcome this, Ruggles provided hinged brace arms on each side of the cylinder. As the rollers passed these arms, they were raised by a cam action, and then dropped back into place. This was rather a complicated arrangement, but was necessary to gain the full advan-

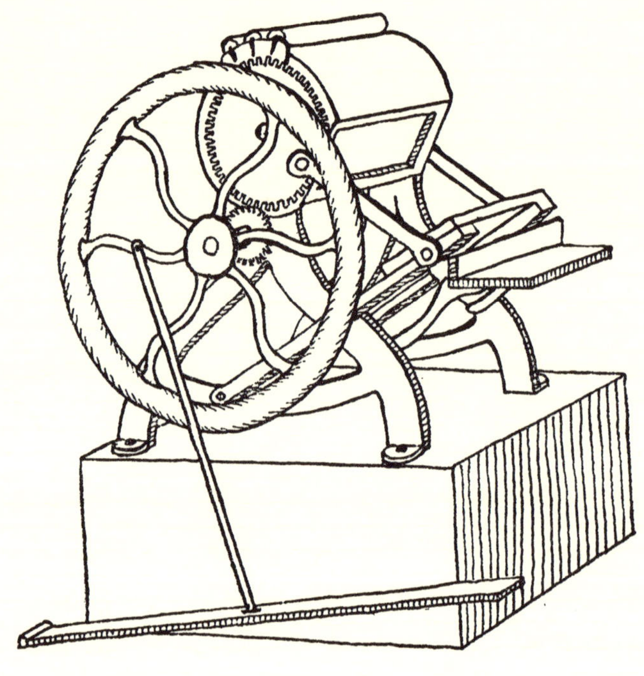

Ruggles' Card and Bill Head Press of 1851

tage of the large ink distribution area. The simple ink disk had not yet appeared.

This was the first real treadle jobber to be regularly manufactured that looked like any of its long list of successors of later years. It had one principal advantage. The paper and type form were always in sight. It was comparatively simple and could be produced at a reasonable price. The chase size of this press was 4½ x 7 inches, and it was advertised as the Card and Bill Head Press.

Within a short time Ruggles brought out two other sizes. The smaller was called the Diamond Card Press with a chase size of only 3 x 4½ inches. It stood on a table and was operated by a hand crank on one side. The other was known as the Job Rotary press and had a 7 x 10 chase.

These small presses were a success and Ruggles went on to larger things. About 1855 he brought out his Combination Job Press, which carried a form about the size of the larger jobbers of today. This was a curious looking press, with a sloping bed and platen. The sheet was carried from the feed table down between the type and platen, and then returned to the feed table. In principle, it was somewhat similar to his first model, the Engine Press, but was larger and not as complicated. Not long after, he made a still larger machine, called the Book and Magazine Press. It was not a success, however. Other and better large presses were already in the field.

About 1857 the Ruggles job presses gave way to the more popular Gordons. Production fell off sharply and at about the end of the Civil War the Ruggles plant ceased to exist. The business had been profitable and Ruggles retired with a fortune estimated at well over half a million. He died at Lisbon, N.Y., in 1880.

There are two or three Ruggles jobbers still in existence, but probably not in use. The printers' magazines of the seventies and eighties listed a great many on the secondhand market. Better presses probably forced them to the junk heap. Devinne reported seeing an Engine Press in operation in New York in the nineties. This press may have had a life of fifty years, but in contrast there are many Gordon presses in out-of-the-way job offices which are over sixty years old and still running almost every day of thc year.

Gordon and his Presses

GEORGE PHINEAS GORDON was born in Salem, N. H. on April 21, 1810. His early education was obtained in the Salem schools and he later attended an academy in Boston. After leaving school he became an actor for a short time and then settled in New York where he learned the printer's trade. Sometime before 1835 he opened his own office.

Gordon was mechanically inclined and during the following fifteen years gave much thought and effort to the construction of a press for job work. His first patent was granted March 26, 1850. This press followed somewhat the same form as the Ruggles Engine Press, but was smaller, and was not upside down. Nothing radically new was embodied in its mechanism and the only claims in the patent covered a method for gripping the sheet and a horizontal traveling brayer roller which served to distribute the ink transversely across a rather large rear roller acting as a distributing table. The construction was not simple.

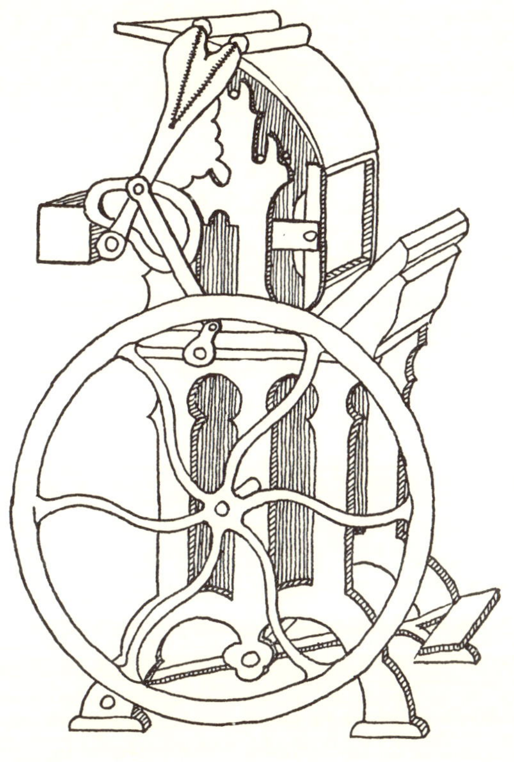

Gordon's "Alligator Press" of 1851

To the best of the writer's knowledge, there are no Gordon presses of this type in existence, and no pictures of this press have ever been found. The patent papers, however, describe the mechanism quite clearly. As this was Gordon's first patent we may infer that the type of press it covered represented the ideas that the inventor had been working on for the preceding fifteen years.

Gordon, in common with all other early job press experimenters, couldn't get away from the hand press principle. Apparently each inventor had the idea that the only possible way to build a power press, was to take an iron hand press, add a self-inking device, and provide some means of mechanically drawing the sheet in and out between the type form and the platen. It seems strange that no one had hit on the simple device of arranging the bed in a vertical position and hinging the lower edge of the platen in front of it.

About this time Ruggles brought out his 1851 press and Gordon at once saw the possibilities of departing from the old hand press scheme. In fact, some years later, Gordon wrote a letter to Ruggles which stated that he was indebted to the latter for the idea of using a vertical bed and hinged platen.

Gordon's next press was the Alligator, brought out sometime in 1851. At least a few were built, but the press was not a success. It does not seem to have been covered by a patent. In principle, it was different. The platen was stationary, and set at an angle of about 45 degrees. The bed, when at rest, was vertical, and hinged at its lower edge. At the proper moment, the bed was tilted forward by a cam device, thru the 45 degree angle, and the form pressed against the platen. Probably a more dangerous piece of apparatus was never built.

The feeder had no warning device to signal to him the necessity for withdrawing his fingers.

An old printer who had operated an Alligator years ago, wrote that Gordon soon realized the dangers in the operation of the press, and immediately bought back the few presses he had sold. It is doubted whether the inventor was charitable to that extent. One Alligator is still in existence in the State Capitol Museum in Lincoln, Nebraska, and woodcuts of this press appeared as late as 1870, indicating that some were still in use and occasionally offered for sale.

Gordon was not losing any time, however. Late in 1851 he was granted a patent which was the basis for all of his later platen jobbers. This patent describes the fundamental features of all later Gordons. The bed of the press was mounted on two legs, which were hinged near the floor, allowing a vibrating motion. The platen was supported by a large shaft, placed in front of the center of area, which allowed a rotating motion of almost 90 degrees. This provided for the typical Gordon action which is still in use today.

The patent sketches and specifications, however, describe a form of mechanism totally different from, and considerably more complicated than the Gordon of later years. Instead of a simple crank action to move the bed back and forth, a toggle affair, actuated by a cam wheel, moved the bed forward at the proper time in the cycle. Another cam wheel moved the platen down from its feeding position to the printing position, much as in later presses, and a third toggle controlled the movements of the roller arms.

Gordon was a spiritualist. He told his friends that Benjamin Franklin had come to him in a dream, for the purpose of describing the new press which Gordon

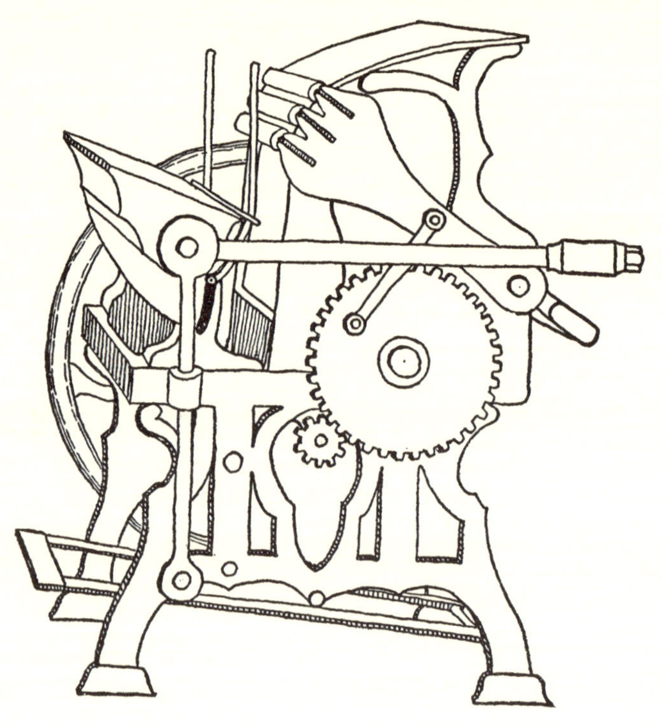

Gordon's "Turnover Press" of 1852

was to make. On the basis of this dream the patent was procured, but Gordon named himself as the inventor.

The press was called the Turnover, due to the novel movement of the platen, which did a partial turnover between the feeding and printing positions. The machine was regularly advertised and probably a number were sold, but within a year or two changes were made both to improve and simplify the mechanism.

Eventually, by 1858, the two extra cam wheels had been eliminated and the press appeared essentially in its final form. In spite of the fact that old Benjamin had described a somewhat imperfect machine to Gordon, the finished product was given the name of the Franklin Press, by the grateful inventor.

In the meantime, during the period from 1853 to 1857, Gordon was selling a new species of fast card press, a patent for which had been granted in 1852. It was called the Firefly, and compared to anything yet produced it really was fast. The speed claimed for it was 8,000 to 10,000 per hour. The stock as fed to the press, was not in the form of individual cards, but was cardboard strip in roll form.

The machine was of the bench type and was operated by a hand crank. After the impression was made, the strip was cut up into individual cards by a shear device, and the cards dropped into a box in the base of the frame. It thereby had automatic feeding and delivery, on the same principle as a web newspaper press, except both type form and platen were flat. The bed had a reciprocating motion, moving backward and forward against the stationary platen like a piston.

Reports indicate that the sale of this press was very profitable, altho for some reason unknown to the writer, the Firefly was not on the market for many years.

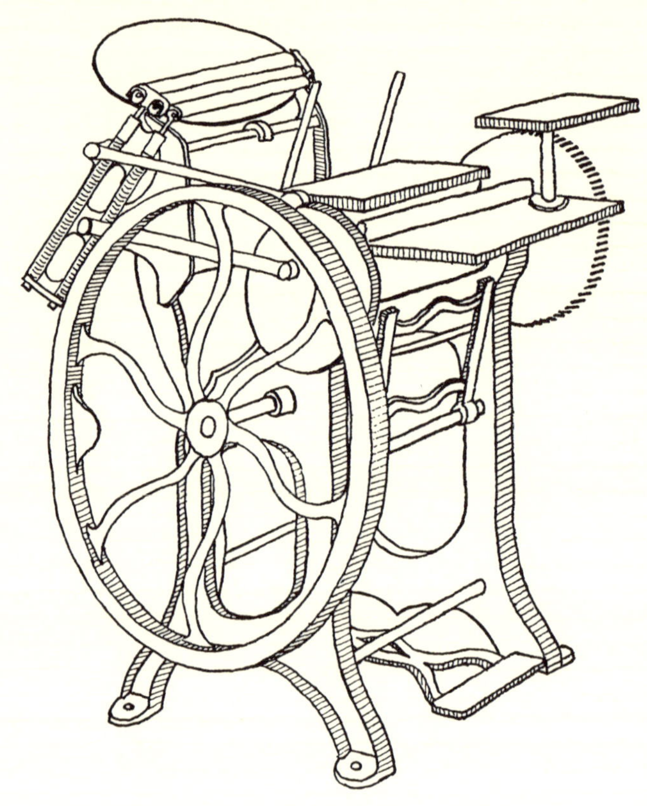

Gordon's "Franklin" of 1863
The typical old-style Gordon of later years

Possibly the grade of work handled by the press was inferior. Not many years ago one of these machines was still in operation in Iowa.

The Ink Disk

ALL OF the small presses made by Gordon and others, up to this time, obtained their ink distribution on a flat or curved ink table. Vibrating rollers were not used and the transverse distribution of the ink across the table was either imperfectly accomplished, or required a complex and expensive roller arrangement. Apparently Gordon and his contemporaries had not thought of the simple revolving ink disk, altho it had been used thirty years before.

Daniel Treadwell, of Boston, was the inventor of the first power printing press to be regularly manufactured in this country and for ink distribution he used a large wooden revolving disk, over which the rollers passed to receive their supply of ink. Possibly fifty Treadwell book presses were made in the 1821 to 1830 period and it seems strange that Gordon may not have seen one. Treadwell, who was in England in the early twenties, probably got his idea from Sir William Congreve's press, which used such an ink disk.

The ink disk as applied to job presses first appears in a patent granted to Gordon in 1856, and which describes a job cylinder press, much like the present Miehle Vertical, but without automatic feeding and delivery. One of the claims in this patent, describes a double ink disk composed of a center circle revolving in one direction with an outer annular ring surrounding it, and revolving in the opposite direction. This, of course, was like the double ink disk later used on the

Chandler & Price Gordons.

Evidently George Gordon knew that the single ink disk was not patentable, but he did conceive the double disk. The vertical cylinder press never appeared on the market, but the double ink disk was used by Gordon on all his subsequent jobbers.

Gordon was certainly a prolific inventor. Patent office records indicate that he was granted almost fifty patents during the period from 1850 to 1875. In addition to the Franklin jobber, Gordon patented a number of small cylinder presses, as well as improved platen jobbers incorporating such ideas as sheet delivery, double ink disks and other features. Some of these presses were on the market a short time but were not successful. The improved Franklin press was the mainstay of the business.

Gordon was not a manufacturer, in the sense that he owned a factory where his presses were produced. The actual manufacture was handled by a number of machine shops, but mostly by a firm in Hope Valley, Rhode Island. In 1872, however, when his presses were at the height of their popularity, Gordon built a factory at Rahway, New Jersey, with a capacity of 600 presses per year.

In the early seventies, Gordon realized that when his patents expired, other press manufacturers would copy the Franklin and the market would be wide open. He therefore conceived the idea of bringing out an entirely new improved press incorporating new principles protected by new patents.

Altho manufacture of this Improved Franklin was started in 1872, the patent was not granted until 1874. The press had about the same general appearance as the old style, but the mechanism for accomplishing the movements of the bed and platen was new. The bed moved thru about half the distance of the old style bed, resulting theoretically in a reduction of power necessary to drive the press. The platen was hinged at its lower edge, instead of in front of its center, and was pushed up to the printing position by a pair of knees.

The press appeared to be somewhat heavier than the old style and had an impression throwoff, the first appearance of this useful item on any of the Gordon jobbers. This was the press that in later years was called the "brass arm Gordon", probably on account of the brass name plate on one of the side arms.

The new style press was not too well received, and there was considerable doubt on the part of printers as to whether it really was an improvement on the old style. The platen didn't open up as far as the platen of the old style. It is the writer's opinion that the popularity of the old style Gordon was due to the accessibility of the tympan surface for make-ready and feeding, and the long rest for feeding in the platen cycle. None of the other jobbers on the market before or since the advent of the old style Gordon had those features so well pronounced, unless possibly the Colts is included, but the Colts was really in a different class.

Gordon suffered from ill health during the last years of his life. At the time of his death he as living in Norfolk, Va., where he had gone to seek s ne improvement. He died January 27, 1878 at the a : of 67, leaving a fortune estimated at almost a million dollars. Although he was known to have made a will, it was not found until twelve years after his death.

In the meantime a number of suits had been started by various relatives and undoubtedly this had an adverse effect on his business. A nephew, A. Sidney Doane, who had worked for Gordon since leaving school, was appointed by the court to manage the business, and continued in this capacity until his death in 1888.

Gordon's prediction that other manufacturers would copy his old style press certainly proved true. Probably the popularity of the old style, and the fact that its manufacture had been discontinued by the Gordon firm, led others into this field.

The final patent applying to improvements on the old style Franklin was granted in 1863, but it wasn't until 1884 that Shneidewend & Lee of Chicago manufactured and sold a copy of the old style. Others quickly followed. Within ten years there were a total of eleven firms manufacturing old style Gordons. Most of them were so like the original Gordon product that it was impossible to tell the difference. Some slight modifications and improvements were made. In general, the later presses were slightly heavier than the Franklin of 1863.

All jobbers in Gordon's time were driven by a foot treadle, and it must have been heavy work to operate one of the larger sizes. It is possible that Gordon aimed at lightness in his presses. They were noted for easy running, compared to some of the other massive productions of the early days of the jobber. For instance, the old wood-cut of the first Cincinnati Type Foundry jobber, which came out just before the Civil War, and which had a great market in the south, showed a slave turning the crank attached to the flywheel.

After 1878, the business was carried on under the name of the Gordon Press Works. No new styles of presses were introduced and competition from other manufacturers was keen. The Government Printing Office was about the only customer to buy the new style in large quantities. After other press makers stole most of the market in the eighties, the Gordon Works again offered the old style press at a competitive price, but in the meantime the business had been on the decline.

In 1901 Chandler & Price, who had been making the old style since 1886, bought out the Gordon Press Works and the right to use the name "Gordon". They continued operating the Rahway plant under the Gordon name, making both the old style and new style presses, until they closed down the factory in 1909. Their original Cleveland plant had, of course, been making an increasing number of old style presses, and presumably the Rahway operation was not profitable.

Altogether there were eighteen different firms making old style Gordons, at one time or another. After 1900 there were only two left. In 1911 the Challenge Machinery Co. discontinued the manufacture of the Challenge Gordon and shortly after the Chandler & Price Co. brought out the New Series press. That marked the end of the old style Gordon, but the New Series press was really the old style with improvements and heavier construction.

Many old style Gordons are in operation today. In fact, if one looks in country printing offices and in smaller shops, the old press seems to be much more common than any other form of jobber. It has been 100 years since Gordon had his dream but in those 100 years the Gordon has been the peer of them all.

The Liberty

THERE WERE many other job platen presses on the market during the second half of the last century. A few others beside the Gordon need special mention. A German, Frederick Otto Degener, worked for Gordon during the latter part of the fifties, and according to his son, was responsible for making the plans from which the Franklin press was built. Degener also had original ideas of his own, and was co-inventor with Gordon, of two of the cylinder jobbers which did not prove successful.

In 1860 Degener procured a patent in his own name and set up in business for himself. The press he invented was called the Liberty and for a short time ran second in popularity to the Gordon. It was a curious sort of press in that the mechanical action was different from any scheme followed before, and never had any imitators.

The platen had about the same kind of motion as the Gordon platen, but the bed, in addition to being supported on legs pivoted at their lower ends, was also hinged or balanced on a shaft running thru the frame in back of the bed. As the platen returned to the feeding position after the impression was made, the bed not only swung backward, as on the Gordon, but also pivoted around a horizontal axis so that the face of the form became horizontal.

The rollers remained in vertical guides and were allowed to move vertically. As the bed pivoted about its axis the disk first passed under the rollers and was followed by the type form. A huge counter-weight was placed in back of the bed which served to balance the load of the bed on its shaft.

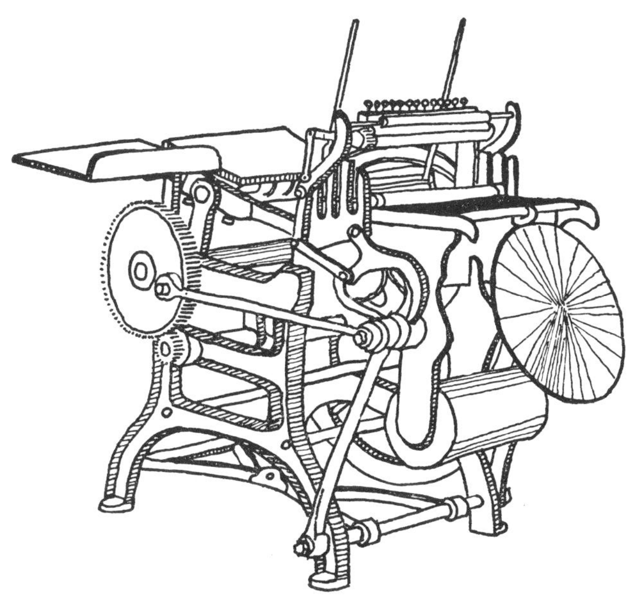

The Liberty of 1870

The Liberty was described as a machine which was half a press long when it was closed up for the impression and two presses long when it opened up and the form was inked. In spite of all this excess movement of its parts, it was reported to run easily without more effort than was needed to "pump" the Gordon. Degener had as a partner, another German named F. M. Weiler and the firm name was Degener & Weiler. Degener died in 1873 and his son, F. L. Degener succeeded him. Weiler bought out the son in 1877 and carried on the business as F. M. Weiler.

About 1881 Weiler established a factory in Berlin, Germany, where his press became popular. The Liberty lost ground in this country, however, and manufacture was discontinued over here in 1890. After that date, the Libertys sold in the United States came from Germany.

Advertisements, under the name of the Liberty Machine Works continued to appear here until 1897. The presses were still on the market in Germany until about the time of World War I.

The Universal

The old hand press principle, as applied to job presses, had one advantage. The bed and platen remained parallel at all times. From 1851 onwards, all jobbers were made with either hinged platens or beds hinged at the lower ends of their supporting legs, so that, when the bed met the platen, the two may not have been exactly parallel. This of course was rectified either by adjustment of the platen, or by adding or withdrawing the packing sheets between the tympan and the platen. Printers realized, however, that for the finest kind of work, parallel impression was desirable.

Merritt Gally, who had at first been a printer, then a clergyman, and finally an inventor, secured a patent in 1863 for a new kind of job press. The frame was massive, heavy, and of one piece box construction. The bed was vertical and fixed. The platen, instead of being hinged, rolled up from its feeding position, until it became vertical and about an inch from the form. From this position it was pulled directly toward the form.

Instead of the customary ink disk, the rollers were supplied by a fountain, and the ink distribution system was located directly above the form. The press, of course, was heavier, slower, and more costly than the Gordon, but with its superior ink distribution and parallel impression, was capable of doing the finest work.

Gally named his press the Universal, and arranged for its manufacture. At first the press was made by Hamilton and McNeal of Rochester, N. Y. Later, John Thompson handled the manufacture and the press was produced at the Colt's Armory plant.

A few years before Gally's patent expired, he and Thompson had a disagreement with the result that Thompson slightly redesigned the press and sold it on his own account under the name of the Colt's Armory press. Gally's ads at the time were full of warnings of dire trouble to buyers of the Colts press, claiming patent infringement.

Evidently the difficulties were either patched up or ignored, because Thompson continued with the sale of his press and Gally had the Universal made elsewhere. Time passed and Gally grew older. No new improvements were made on the Universal, and after Gally's death in 1910, the business was carried on as the National Machine Co. The Colts press however, was pushed much more energetically and remains a good press today. In 1923 the National Machine Co. combined with the John Thompson Co. to form the Thompson-National Press Co. The firm makes more cutting and creasing presses than printing machines. The Colts was never equipped with automatic feeding, so it has always been a slow press, but capable of excellent work.

The Clamshell Press

IN THE seventies and eighties, when job press manufacture was booming and many small firms entered the field, the business became highly competitive. Small offices and country printers wanted job presses but didn't always have the money for the outlay. For this type of customer, a light, cheap press was devised, and made at different times and places by a number of machine shops and small factories.

This particular species of press was afterwards designated as the clamshell. The bed and frame were made in one fixed assembly and the platen rocked back and forth on hinges attached to its lower side. The mechanism was as simple as possible, and as the platen rocked back and forth with uniform motion, there was no rest or stopping of its movement for feeding.

Some of these presses were made by unknown manufacturers who furnished them to printers' supply houses, to be labeled and advertised as the product of the firm selling them. Thus the same identical make of press was sold under two or three different names, in different parts of the country.

In all cases these clamshell presses were light in construction and were not long-lived. Most of them were

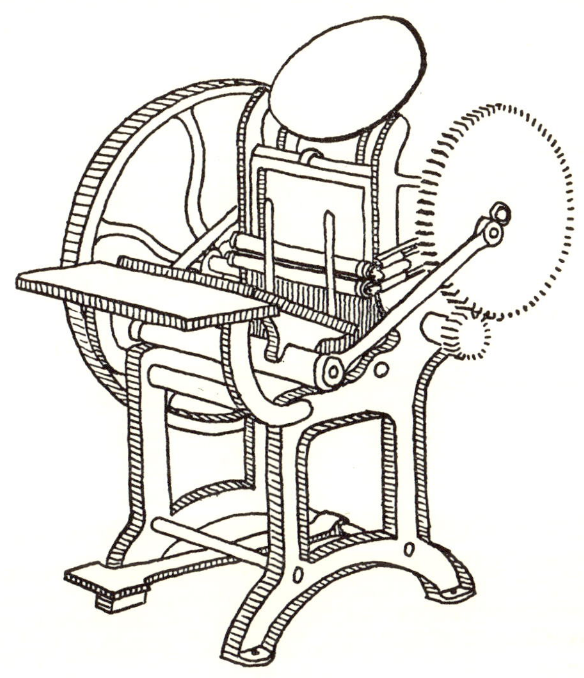

Typical Clamshell Press of 1880

on the market but a few years. About all they offered to the history of job press manufacture was a great confusion of names.

Other Jobbers

IN ADDITION to the jobbers already mentioned, there were a few good presses which have been almost forgotten due to the overshadowing popularity of the Gordon. John M. Jones of Palmyra, N. Y., who built presses from 1868 to about 1902, produced nine different styles, among them the Globe, Star, Peerless and Lightning. He also fell in line and made an old style Gordon, sold under the name of the Jones-Gordon.

The Cincinnati Type Foundry made jobbers from 1855 until about 1885, at first called the Wells, and later the Nonpareil. R. Hoe & Co. made two or three styles in the fifties and sixties but couldn't stand the competition, so withdrew.

Probably the best known of the later crop was the Golding, which first came out in 1874 and lasted until 1927. The small, light weight Pearl was also made by the same company, thruout the same span of over fifty years.

The Impression Throwoff

FOR THE benefit of the uninformed, the impression throwoff is a very useful adjunct to a job press which limits the motion of the platen when the pressman misses a sheet, so that the type won't print on the bare tympan sheet. It is operated by a lever at the left hand side of the press, between the platen and the flywheel. This lever may be very quickly and easily pushed forward, almost at the last second before the impression is made.

If the press is power operated, and it is desired to miss a few impressions without stopping the press, the throwoff may also be used as a temporary means of preventing the press from printing until the pressman resumes feeding.

Most of the earlier jobbers did not have throwoffs. In the case of a small treadle driven press, it probably was not considered the absolute necessity that it is to-day, as if a sheet was missed or incorrectly placed on the tympan, the press could usually be stopped in time. The first appearance of the throwoff was in a patent covering improvements to printing presses issued to James Young, of Philadelphia, in 1852.

Nothing is known of any presses made by Young but only a year later, a patent procured by Ruggles illustrates and describes a similar throwoff, but does not include it as one of the claims. Possibly Ruggles had made arrangements to use the Young throwoff. The next appearance of the throwoff was on the Liberty press.

One of Degener's patents clearly indicates the throw-off mechanism and lists it as one of the claims. The eccentric mechanism, however, instead of being a part of the front platen shaft, as on the Young press, was a part of the main rear shaft which supported the bed. The operating levers performed their function in a somewhat different manner, so conceivably the Degener claim was not an infringement of Young's rather narrow claims.

Gordon did not provide a throwoff on any of his original old-style presses. Possibly he had made unsuccessful attempts to design some mechanism to accomplish the same purpose, but certainly none of his patent papers or early advertisements indicate in any way that a throwoff was part of his presses.

In 1872, however, when Gordon brought out his new style press, the Young patent had expired and a throwoff was provided. The design of this press was such that a throwoff of the typical, or Young type, could be applied very easily. In the case of the old-style Gordon, the design did not lend itself to the easy application of a throwoff.

Shortly after Shniedewend & Lee started making old-style Gordons in the early eighties, a workman of theirs, H. F. Bechman, devised a throwoff with the eccentric located on the rear shaft. The patent covering this arrangement however, was not broad enough to prevent other Gordon press makers from applying somewhat similar schemes, and shortly afterwards, all Gordons could be bought with or without throwoffs. Some old-styles were manufactured without throwoffs as late as the turn of the century.

The Decline and Fall
of the Treadle Jobber

DURING the hundred year period from 1840 to 1940, there were at least 123 different treadle driven, hand fed platen jobbers manufactured in this country. In some cases, of course, certain makers, such as Jones of Palmyra, built two or more styles, each with a different name.

Of these 123 different advertised names, there were 56 Clam Shell presses, 18 old-style Gordons, 9 of the type made by the Cincinnati Type Foundry with long front hinge, 8 with parallel impression, such as the Colts, 6 with cylindrical bed like the 1851 Ruggles

press, 2 new-style Gordons and 24 others of miscellaneous types such as the Liberty, Golding and many
others.

The height of the jobber building activity occurred
in 1888 when there were 36 different makes of presses
being manufactured. From that date there was a steady
decline in the variety until 1900 when only 16 kinds
were on the market.

Today only the Chandler & Price Gordon, the Colts,
and one or two copies of smaller presses are still being
manufactured. The hand fed jobber, except for small
runs, is no longer economical.

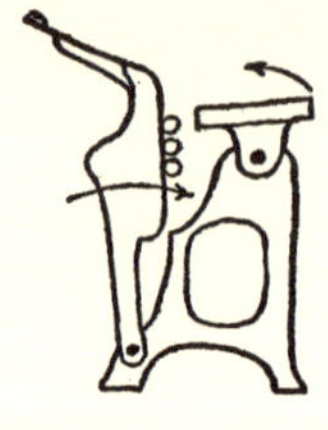

a. Old Style Gordon

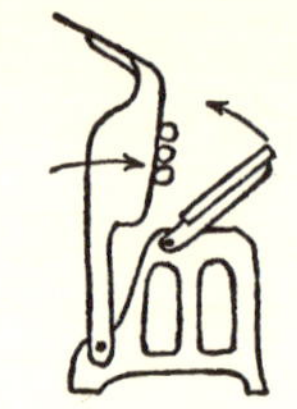

b. New Style Gordon

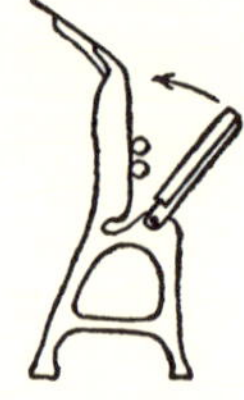

c. Simple Clamshell Press

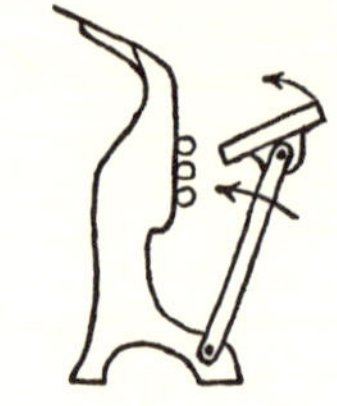

d. Platen Pivoted on Long
Front Legs

e. Parallel Impression

f. Cylindrical Bed

Major Types of Job Platen Presses

THE following table lists all the makers of platen treadle-driven jobbers of which the writer has record. The dates indicate the known years during which the press was manufactured, altho in a large percentage of cases, the press was probably on the market for a greater period than is indicated. Not all of the clamshell type, marked "c" in the table, were of the simple, light, cheap type. A great many of this group, such as the Golding and Peerless, were good presses of durable construction, and were arranged with cams or other devices to allow for a rest for feeding. The following letters have been used to indicate the mechanical action or type of press.

a. Old style Gordon
b. New style Gordon.
c. Bed fixed and platen pivoted at lower edge (clam shell)
d. Bed fixed and platen supports pivoted near floor, with platen pivoted at its center.
e. Parallel impression, like the Colts.
f. With cylindrical bed, like the Ruggles
g. Other types.

Adams	g 1853-59	Adams Press Works, Boston
	1859-73	R. Hoe & Co., New York
Aldine	c 1878	Dokum & Sons, New York
Aldine	d 1874-5	B. F. Renick & Co., Canton, O.
Alert	c 1878-80	W. B. Gorham & Co., Boston
Allen	f 1873	Allen Mfg. Co., Norwich, Conn.
Allen	c 1884	Allen Mfg. Co., Norwich, Conn.
Allen	c 1929	L. F. Grammes & Sons, Allentown, Pa.
Alligator	g 1851	Geo. P. Gordon, New York
American	e 1877-82	J. E. Braunsdorf, New York
American	c 1886	Sold thru dealers
Asteroid	d 1875	Cincinnati Type Foundry
Atlas	? 1885	Sold thru dealers
Baltimore	c 1880-95	J. F. W. Dorman, Baltimore
Ben Franklin	a 1886-98	Johnson-Peerless Works, Palmyra, N. Y.
Bronson	a 1894-7	H. Bronson, Chicago
California Reliable	a 1886-9	Palmer & Rey, San Francisco
Caxton	g 1861-5	R. Hoe & Co., New York
Challenge	a 1884-93	Shniedewend & Lee, Chicago
	a 1894-10	Challenge Machinery Co., Grand Haven, Mich.
Chandler & Price	a 1886-53	Chandler & Price, Cleveland
Chromatic	d 1871-3	Suitterlin & Claussen, Chicago
City Jobber	c 1892	Sold thru dealers
Cleveland	a 1890-5	Cleveland-Gordon Press Co., Cleveland
Clipper	c 1881-9	Globe Mfg. Co., Palmyra, N. Y.
C.M.C.	c 1936-50	Craftsmen Mchry. Co., Boston

Colts Armory e 1885-1923 John Thompson, Hartford,
                        Conn.
Columbian   g 1878-91 Curtis & Mitchell, Boston
Damon &
  Peets   b 1892-00 Damon & Peets, New York
               1900-08 Geo. Damon & Sons, New York
Dauntless   c 1882-93 P. J. Jennings, New York
Day   g 1859-64 W. T. & S. D. Day & Co.,
                        Cincinnati
Degener   g 1879-82 Degener & Clash, New York
Diamond   f 1851-65 S. P. Ruggles Power Press Mfg.
                        Co., Boston
Dodson   a 1948-53 Dodson's Printers Supply Co.,
                        Atlanta
Eagle   c 1884-98 Sold thru dealers
Eclipse   g 1884-95 J. F. W. Dorman, Baltimore
Elm City   c   Same as Clipper
Empire   c 1875-8   W. B. Gorham & Co., Boston
Engine   e 1840-65 S. P. Ruggles Power Press Mfg.
                        Co., Boston
Eureka   d 1872-80 A. & B. Newbury, Coxsackie,
                        N. Y.
Evans   c 1875-80 W. C. Evans, Philadelphia
Excelsior   g 1868-70 Wm. Braidwood, New York
Excelsior   c 1878-86 Kelsey & Co., Meriden, Conn.
Favorite   c 1887-94 Damon & Peets, New York
Franklin   a 1855-72 Geo. P. Gordon, New York
             b 1873-09 Gordon Press Works, New York
Giles Ideal c 1935   Ideal Printers Supply Co.,
                        Chicago
Gilman   e 1844   Alonzo Gilman, Troy, N. Y.
               1846-73 R. Hoe & Co., New York
Globe   g 1869-76 J. M. Jones, Palmyra, N. Y.

Golden Gate	c		Sold thru dealers in California
Golding	g	1874-27	Golding Mfg. Co., Boston
Gordon			See Franklin
Hartford	e		Same as Colts Armory
Harvard	c	1883	Robson & Loughry, Boston
Hercules	g	1876	?
Hoe	g	1864-6	R. Hoe & Co., New York
Imperial	d	1905	Imperial Art Press Co., Boston
Jewell	c	1881-9	Globe Mfg. Co., Palmyra, N. Y.
		1890-1	Johnson-Peerless Works, Palmyra, N. Y.
Jones-Gordon	a	1888-01	John M. Jones Co., Palmyra, N.Y.
		1901-2	Jones-Gordon Press Works, Palmyra, N. Y.
Kidder	g	1874-9	Standard Machry. Co. Dover, N. H.
King	c	1911-38	Kelsey Press Co., Meriden, Conn.
Lawyer	c	1857-64	Geo. H. Lawyer, Cincinnati
Leader	c	1881-3	J. M. Jones, Palmyra, N. Y.
Liberty	g	1860-77	Degener & Weiler, New York
		1877-90	F. M. Weiler, New York
		1890-97	Liberty Machine Works, New York
Lightning	c	1896-01	J. M. Jones Co., Palmyra, N. Y.
		1901-3	Jones-Gordon Press Works, Palmyra, N. Y.
Lion	g	1851-8	Chas. W. Hawkes, Boston
Madison	a	1890-2	W. G. Walker & Co., Madison, Wis.
Model	c	1877-85	J. W. Daughaday & Co., Philadelphia
		1886-05	Model Press Co., York, Pa.
Monarch	f	1880	Griffith & Byrne, New York

Monumental	c 1876-93	J. F. W. Dorman, Baltimore
Monitor	c 1875-9	Monitor Press Co., New York
National	f 1873	Allen Mfg. Co., Norwich, Conn.
National	c 1880-83	National Printers Warehouse, New York
National	e 1910-23	National Machine Co., Hartford, Conn.
New Champion	c 1886-8	A. Olmesdahl, New York
	1889-00	New Champion Press Co. New York
New Era	a 1894	J. M. Jones Co., Palmyra, N. Y.
New York	c 1876-7	M. L. Gump, New York
Nonpareil	d 1868-85	Cincinnati Type Foundry
Novelty	c 1877-80	Benj. O. Woods, Boston
Official	c 1881-93	Golding Mfg. Co., Boston
O.K.	c 1886-98	Kelsey Press Co., Meriden, Conn.
Old Reliable	a 1888	H. H. Thorp Mfg. Co., Cleveland
Paragon	d 1878	S. P. Rounds, Chicago
Pearl	c 1876-1927	Golding Mfg. Co., Boston
Peerless	c 1875-1818	Globe Mfg. Co., Palmyra, N.Y.
Peerless-Gordon	a 1891-1900	Peerless Printing Press Co., Palmyra, N. Y.
Phenix	c 1876-81	Empire Press Co., Coxsackie, N. Y.
Pioneer	c 1880	Miss. Type Co., Grenada, Miss.
Potter	g 1858-66	C. Potter Jr., Westerly, R. I.
Powell	a 1884	F. M. Powell & Co., Chicago
Premier	c 1886	Joseph Watson, New York
Priest	f 1860	J. E. Priest, St. Louis
Prouty	c 1878-1926	Geo. W. Prouty & Co., Boston
Reliable	d 1882-93	Cincinnati Type Foundry

Reliable	c 1880	A. Newbury, Coxsackie, N. Y.
Ruggles		See Diamond and Engine
Samson	c 1885-95	Joseph Watson, New York
S. & L.	a 1884-93	Shniedewend & Lee, Chicago
Standard	c 1876-81	H. H. Thorp Mfg. Co., Cleveland
Star	c 1875-89	J. M. Jones Co., Palmyra, N. Y.
Star	c 1901-53	Kelsey Press Co., Meriden, Conn.
Straight Line Gordon	a 1891	Thos. Holliday, Chicago
Superior	c 1879-82	E. Remington & Sons, New York
Taylor	f 1871-3	A. B. Taylor Pr. Press & Machry. Co., New York
Thorp-Gordon	a 1886-90	H. H. Thorp Mfg. Co., Cleveland
Union	c 1898-1939	Kelsey Press Co., Meriden, Conn.
United States	c 1877-95	Joseph Watson, New York
Universal	e 1869-1910	Merritt Gally, New York
Up-to-Date	c 1898-9	Victor Press Co., New York
Washington	g 1869	Thos. H. Senior, New York
Washington	c 1880-9	J. M. Jones Co., Palmyra, N. Y.
Wells	d 1855-68	Cincinnati Type Foundry
Willard's Noiseless	g 1891	Fred G. Willard, Chicago
Yorkston	c 1872-7	M. L. Gump, New York
Young America	c 1880	Joseph Watson, New York

Of four hundred and ninety-five copies of this book, printed at the Printing Office of Philip Reed,

this is number

ON MAKING A PRINTING PRESS

by RALPH GREEN

ON MAKING A PRINTING PRESS

SOME twenty years ago, when I had occasion to study old wooden printing press construction, I was impressed by the ability of the artisans of that day, to make a printing press with so few tools, and probably not good tools at that. Wooden printing presses were built long before the introduction of machine tools. The hand tools available were those of the carpenter and blacksmith. Some ingenuity and a great deal of slow, painstaking labor was necessary to cut the threads of the screw of the spindle. Other parts were easy to make.

If it were possible to make such a press with hand tools, why couldn't I? I had a workshop, with all the usual hand tools and such skill as the average amateur might possess. Moreover, I had been without a press since my school days, and I thought it would be fun to own one again.

I decided that a platen and chase size of 6 by 9 inches would do for eveything I wanted to print. Unfortunately I had not run across anything in the literature of printing which would give me any indication of the required pressure to be exerted by the platen. I am a structural engineer and intended to design each part for a definite loading, so like the one-horse shay, under an overload, all parts would break at once. For such a small chase size, I decided that 1500 pounds pressure would be sufficient and made my plans accordingly. This was equivalent to about 28 pounds per square inch of platen area, and I was to learn later that a design unit load of from two to three times that figure should be used for a good strong hand press with the ability to print a full form. However,

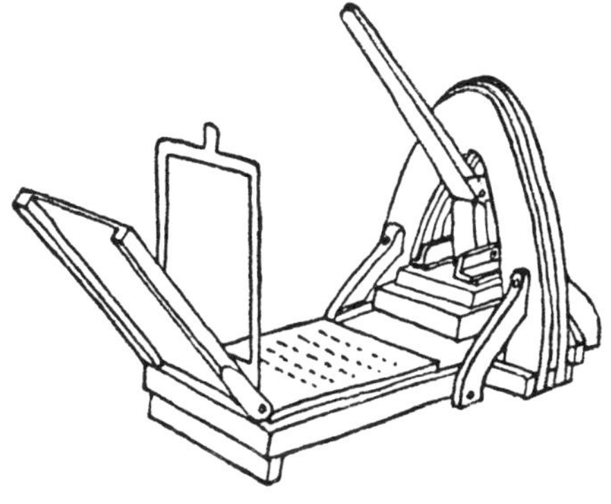

the press as built seemed to be of ample strength, although I have probably over-loaded it at times.

Most of the press was made of oak, reen-forced with steel bars and held together by bolts. I was fortunate in obtaining a piece of lightweight steel plate, with a polished finish on both sides, which I used for the underside of the wooden platen. Instead of using a screw for the spindle, which would have been proper for an eighteenth century press, I used the far more efficient toggle joint, thus placing the press in the 1815 - 1825 period. For the bed of the press I used a piece of hard Masonite, supported by a flat oak surface. I dispensed with the rounce and girt straps, as the bed could be moved in and out easily by hand. Much to my surprise, the press worked quite satisfactorily and required little make ready.

In using the press, I learned a few things about the operation of a hand press, or at least about this particular press. With almost any small form, even tho it was only slightly off center, it was necessary to place a bearer in the opposite end of the chase, so that the impression would be even and

[4]

square. I had a few old cuts of assorted sizes, which I used for this purpose and which were turned face down in the form.

To insure even inking with a hand roller I soon discovered it was necessary to use some form of roller bearers. For this purpose I devised a light frame, of the proper thickness, and large enough to enclose the form, yet narrow enough to support the ends of the roller. This was placed on the form during the inking process, and removed before the tympan was closed down on the form. I soon worked out an efficient technique for handling the bearer, ink slab, roller, paper, frisket, tympan, bed and bar handle, each in turn, and was able to print at the rate of 300 per hour, or slightly better. Of course this rate could be maintained for short bursts of speed only.

This press was not large enough or strong enough to print anything of consequence, and I was limited to small items such as cards, stationery, announcements etc. A run of 300 or more involved too much time and effort, and the operation of the press, when the novelty wore off, ceased to be a pleasure if a run of more than 100 was involved. The next, and most logical step, was the making of a self-inking press, to take care of the longer runs of the smaller items. Accordingly I made plans for a typical amateur press with vertical bed and revolving ink disk. I designed this press for a unit pressure of about 80 pounds per square inch of chase area, which proved to be ample. However, as most of the frame was wood, and as the main members had to be somewhat bulky to withstand the stresses, the maximum chase area was limited to 25 square inches, or slightly more than 4x6. It took about six months of my spare time to make this press, and again, it was made with ordinary hand tools. The bearings, of course, were metal, and there was quite a bit of iron bar reenforcing, with some parts made of pipe and pipe fittings. I even made the ink disk. This was made of wood, covered with polished sheet steel,

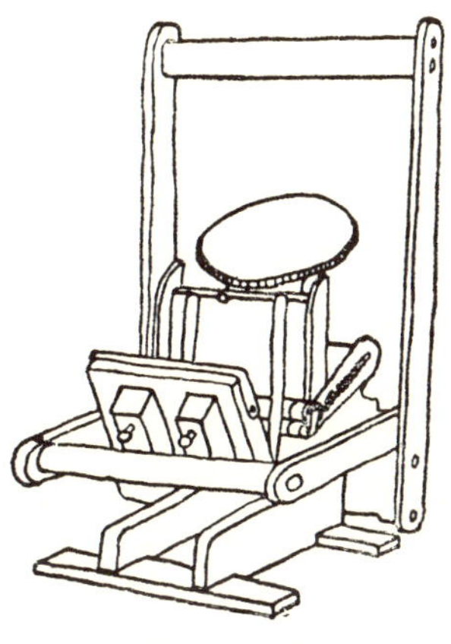

and the ratchet teeth were cut out of a circle of thin band iron. The principle of operation was much like that of the Pilot press, with fairly heavy side arms. Instead of one side lever, however, I used two, one on each side, with a connecting bar across the top. I incorporated one or two improvements. A large spiral spring (it was a valve spring from an old gas engine) combined with a piece of foam rubber, made an excellent shock absorber when the lever was released, and the press was so designed that the platen opened up more, and its lower edge was further from the ink rollers than is the case with other amateur presses of its size. In size, it took up more space than an iron press of twice its chase area.

For small work this press was quite successful. It was better balanced, easier to operate, and faster than any press of its size I had ever handled. It had one failing. In the course of time the wooden parts shrunk slightly, or otherwise got out of line. Knowing its construction thoroughly, however, I could make satisfactory adjustments whenever necessary.

This press was far too small, however,

and I wanted a press large enough to print two pages at a time. Speed was secondary as I didn't plan to print many copies. I decided a good strong hand press of the Washington type and about 10x15 chase size would be sufficiently large. Furthermore, it is possible to print a form of almost the full size of the chase on a hand press of the Washington type. This is not possible with a self-inking press employing an ink disk, as approximately the center seven-tenths only, of the form, receives perfect inking. Roughly speaking, the extent of good inking is about equal to half of the area of the chase, or somewhat less than the area of a square which can be placed within the outline of the ink disk.

I made plans for a press to be made of wood, iron, wrought pipe, brass, and other miscellaneous materials. It was a cross between a Washington hand press and a Rube Goldberg concoction. Unfortunately, the late war had started before my plans were finished, and I found that (a) I didn't have the time to spend in my workshop, and (b) I couldn't get materials. There were priorities required for everything. I had to give the idea up.

Later, I had a chance to buy a 6 x 9 Sigwalt. This was a nice little amateur type self-inking press, and it operated quite satisfactorily. It wasn't large enough to print a sizable sheet, however.

About a year ago I saw an advertisement offering an 8x12 Golding hand press. I had known that amateur presses of this comparatively large size were made in the past; in fact, I had pictures of them and two old Golding catalogs showing the full line. This press turned out to be the rather rare type made for printing notes on large drawings and similar work. The platen is fixed and almost horizontal. The entire upper part of the press consisting of bed, ink disk, roller arms, etc., is hinged at its lower edge. When the long side lever is pulled down, most of the machine bends over, to make the impression on the platen, and if you are standing close to it you get the impression that the ink disk is about to hit you in the face. Two large strong springs on either side control the movement and make it surprisingly easy to operate. The lettering on the side of the bed, "Golding & Co., Boston," indicates that the press is about 55 years old.

I bought the press, took it apart, gave it a good cleaning, polished up the bright surfaces, and gave it two coats of enamel. After this treatment it looked as good as new. This is the press I have now.

Some five years ago, when Colonial Williamsburg established their 18th century printing office, I had the pleasure of preparing the detail plans of the Common

English Press which is now in use in the shop. The press is a composite of four 18th century presses in museums in this country supplemented by such data as I had acquired from twenty years study of the subject. Amateurs with a strong desire to build a press have corresponded with me and discussed the feasability of making a wood press with an iron screw, similar to the 1750 - 1815 style. I have discouraged the making of a press of this exact type. The screw would be difficult to cut for any machine shop, as it has a very coarse thread with a descent of over two inches in one revolution. Furthermore, the operation of a screw press is inefficient and would be very tiring. An adaptation of the toggle joint, to suit materials and methods available to the amateur, would be much easier of accomplishment, and would result in a more efficient and easier operating press. It would be much more powerful than the screw spindle; in fact, there would be some danger of weakening the frame of the press.

In England in the early days of the last century, after Charles, third Earl Stanhope had invented the first iron press by combining the toggle joint with the screw, some English press makers continued to make wooden presses, but with the Stanhope mechanism. The idea was not entirely successful, as the toggle joint exerted so much power, the wooden frames, in many instances, could not withstand the pressure. However, in those days, the method of figuring exact stresses in the timber work was unknown and the frames were not provided with sufficient strength to take an exact maximum platen pressure. If a small, heavy wooden press were designed for a known platen pressure, no such difficulty should result.

Of course, if the amateur had the facilities of a metal working shop, with welding equipment, he could make his press entirely of iron and steel. He would save much time and money, however, if he scoured the second hand market and found an old Washington at a reasonable price.

If an amateur wanted a press with a comparatively large chase size, and wasn't too

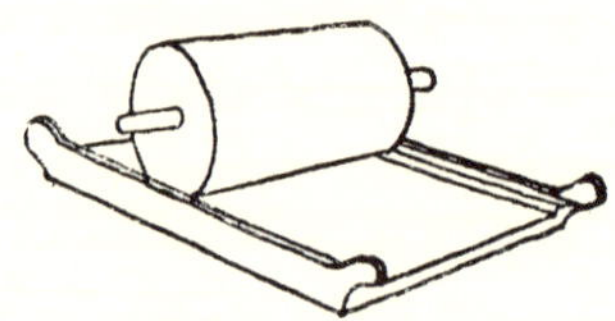

particular about the quality of his press work, he might well consider a galley proof press. A great many were made in the past and are still on the market. They have a bed size of about 10 x 30 or larger. They are simple, hand operated cylinders, about nine inches in diameter, running on iron rails on an iron bed. They would, of course, require hand inking with a brayer, and in speed of operation may be slightly faster than a Washington. Some means would have to be provided for getting good register, but by the exercise of some ingenuity this could be worked out.

It may be interesting to recall at this point, that the first amateur presses regularly made and sold in this country were of the cylinder type. The Lowe, with conical shaped roller, was patented in 1856. Ben Grauer, of NBC, has one and uses it occasionally. The Adams Cottage Press, similar to a simple proof press but with the cylinder fixed and a sliding bed, appeared in 1860. Amateur platen presses with vertical beds were not made before 1869.

A number of years ago you could buy for fifty cents, instructions for making a press. The press was of the proof press type, with the roller made of a round

Quaker Oats box filled with concrete, and a piece of broom stick through it to serve as a handle. The bed and cylinder bearers were to be made of hard wood. A specimen printed on this press indicated that it would at least print, but the quality of the press work left much to be desired.

Art stores sell a simple contraption made of wood and iron, for use in printing linoleum blocks. A quick study of the probable strength of the mechanism leaves you wondering how it can possibly exert any appreciable force between the block and the platen. Linoleum blocks usually have masses of dark areas, requiring two or three times as much platen pressure as solid type matter. Maybe the users are satisfied with a gray, speckled impression. One of these presses may serve as a good example of what not to do when building a small, serviceable, strong press.

Probably a better, makeshift press for

printing linoleum blocks, as well as type matter, consists of an old iron letter press with screw-down platen actuated by a wheel or bar at the top. The writer once saw one of these arranged with a sliding bed, tympan and frisket, and provided with a larger iron wheel at the top. It appeared to be operating satisfactorily, altho it was slower, and more force was required than if it had been a toggle joint press.

An article in an early issue of the Saint Nicholas magazine described a press made by a country boy who had acquired some type thrown out by the local newspaper. He used a heavy plank about twelve inches wide by five feet long. About nine inches of one end constituted the bed, on which was placed the chase. Above this the platen was hinged to the end of the plank. An iron strap arrangement surrounded the bed and platen, and between this strap and the platen was inserted a 2 by 4 about four

feet long. A block attached to the top of
the platen was so located that the leverage
ratio was about 50 to 1. A force of about
40 pounds applied to the bar handle exerted a pressure of 2000 pounds on the
platen, which was enough for the purpose.

An English text book on the subject of
printing in the schools, contains sketches
of a somewhat similar, but obviously less
powerful, homemade press.

And this concludes my remarks on the
making of a printing press. If you have a
desire to make such a press, I wish you
luck. You will have a lot of fun, and if
the press works, an immense satisfaction.

170 Copies
Hand Set
Printed
& Bound
by the Author

1 9 5 5